This Will Help You Grow

Advice and Encouragement
for Suzuki Parents

by Brittany P. Gardner

Dedication

To Mr. Aaron, for teaching me week after week, lesson after lesson, how to believe in my own capabilities

To Mrs. Moench, for teaching me week after week, lesson after lesson, how to believe in my child's capabilities

Table of Contents

Foreword: Don't Take Anyone's Advice

This may seem like a strange title for the forward of a book that is full of advice and encouragement. I mean, if you've picked up this book, then you probably *are* searching for advice. And encouragement. And some kind of help or list of ideas that will ease your struggle, or infuse your journey with a little more joy. And that truly is what I've set out to do.

But if I'm intent on sharing my experience and advice, gleaned over two decades of teaching and over a decade of being a music parent, why would I begin a book full of advice with the injunction to *not* take anyone's advice?

Let me explain.

When I was pregnant with my first child, I was determined to learn all I could about this new phase of life I was about to enter, called "motherhood."

I have always been a hard worker, a problem-solver, a go-getter. Through my own life's experiences, I have learned, and learned well, that any difficulty can be overcome if you just have the right plan, the right perseverance, and the right support. This worked for me when I was taking calculus classes in school, preparing for high-stakes music auditions, applying to college, deciding which career path to pursue, figuring out my place in a community. I figured the same approach would serve me just as well in this new undertaking of becoming a parent.

When it came to motherhood, I figured I would employ my usual tactics of problem-solving: I would be prepared, and I would be informed, and I would create a plan, and I would follow that plan, and I would be successful.

And so I took those problem-solving, go-getting skills right with me into pregnancy. I read every parenting book I could get my hands on. I watched helpful videos and talked to seasoned parents. I took notes. I made plans. I crafted schedules (for a baby who was yet to be born!). I got my data and charts and information all lined up so that I could be prepared. Because present preparation meant future success. (right?)

So imagine my surprise one day when, while at a baby shower, I heard words that contradicted all my diligent preparation.

The guests were all sitting in a circle, taking turns offering words of wisdom to me, the mother-to-be.

And let me tell you, I got some great advice!

Sleep when the baby sleeps. Take care of yourself. Reach out for help. Make sure you get outside. Remember your child is not you, and will come with her own personality.

Fabulous wisdom that I couldn't write down fast enough in my expectant mother notebook!

And then it came time for my brother-in-law, Josh, to share his advice with me. Josh, a father of three, had always been someone whose wisdom I respected. He'd often patiently talked with me and given thoughtful counsel when I sought it from him, and he had led a life full of purpose and care. So I was very anxious to soak in all the wisdom he had to offer.

Before he spoke, he paused, slightly tilted his head, and then finally said, "My advice? Don't take anyone's advice."

What? How could I write that down in my notebook? Where did that fit in my table of data and pages of information? Did he mean my pages and pages of notes should be thrown out the window?

How could that even be helpful? You mean all my researching and reading and asking and questioning was all in vain? *What do you even mean?*

Being the inquisitive, problem-solver that I am, I asked him exactly that. "Josh, what do you even mean?"

He replied, "All the reading and research and asking and listening is good. It allows you to be informed and educated; to see what is out there. But at the end of the day, your life is your own. The way you parent is your own. You will know better than any other human being how to nurture and raise this child that is about to come in to your life. At first you won't believe or understand that, but that wisdom will come with time and experience. Don't outsource this privilege, and don't budge when someone tells you to do something that, in your gut, you feel isn't right for you and your family."

Clearly, because I'm writing this for you to read twelve years after it happened, this incident had a profound effect on me. Since that day, I have continued to do my best to read, research, ask, listen and become well-informed. But when it comes down to it, to making the big decisions on how best to raise my child and guide my family, I have always taken Josh's advice, and turned inward to my intuition.

I invite you to do the same.

Maybe you're a new music parent wondering how to get started. Maybe you're a seasoned parent who's facing burn out. Maybe you're a parent who has graduated from the intensive child-rearing years and who is looking back wondering, did I do the right things? Maybe you're somewhere in between all of those places.

But the reality is, if you've read this far into this book, then something in you is probably searching for some new ideas, advice, reassurance, and hope. And I guarantee I can offer at least some of those things to some of my readers, especially those who read with an open heart.

What I *don't* guarantee is a play book on how to rear your child, how to avoid heartache or mistakes, how to have practice sessions that are always peaceful and cooperative, how to reach the same level of success as your neighbor or friend or third cousin twice removed. Your journey is your own. As a parent, as a person, as a human.

And so is your child's.

This book is not intended to necessarily be read in any kind of order; the writings are not organized in any specific sequence, which, if followed, will guarantee you success. Rather, it is meant to be used as a reference or guide book for you as a parent as you walk along the music pathway with your child.

If you are wondering about a particular theme or struggle of your journey, I hope you look it up in the table of contents and head directly there! It is my hope that you find a nugget of wisdom here or there that aids you in strengthening your relationship with your child, or easing your music journey together, or finding joy in your efforts. I hope also that you realize you are not alone in your quest to better your family's life through music study.

Each section is followed by a practice; a set of exercises, usually very simple, that will guide you to a deeper understanding and deeper skill in your role as a music parent. I am, after all, a music teacher, and as such, I believe deeply in the concept of practicing and repeating a skill until it becomes engrained in our souls. As Dr. Suzuki said, "Ability equals knowledge plus 10,000 times." That is true for any skill we wish to develop, be it mastery of a musical instrument or a greater level of patience as a parent.

It's the conscientious repetition of 10,000 times that takes a skill from our *brain* and deeply roots it within our *hearts*.

If we want our children to learn this vital skill, of being changed through practice, can we not commit to developing it ourselves? Can we be vulnerable enough to change through practice? Can we repeat the skill 10,000 times so that it moves from our brain into our hearts?

I believe we can.

So, let's begin.

Introduction: This Will Help You Grow

Like many of my colleagues, I have spent time in all three corners of the Suzuki Triangle. I was a Suzuki student first and have been a Suzuki teacher for almost twenty years. I've also been a Suzuki parent for nine years, and I can tell you that while my time in the parent corner has been shorter than my time in the other two corners, my *growth* from that vantage point has been the most transformative. I want to share some insights with you that I've had as a teacher first and a parent second that have been helpful to me as I've been working with my children.

Before I talk about some specifics, I want to share one crucial difference I've found in the perspective between the teacher and the parent. That is, when a student comes to me for a lesson, they walk in the studio and all I see is possibility. I don't know their full story. I don't know the problems in their life or the challenges they may be facing. I don't know what their limitations are. All I see is a child full of potential, and I see where we can go together, how we can grow, what goals we can reach together. It is a wonderful privilege as a teacher to see a child's limitless, unencumbered potential in front of me.

On the other hand; as a parent you know the whole story. You know what's going on right now in your child's life. You know what difficulties they have; you know what struggles they've overcome. You have walked with them every bit of the way and helped carry those struggles and difficulties.

Before you read any further, stop and thank yourself. Extend mercy and gratitude to yourself for being there as a partner with and champion for your child, however imperfect you may feel. You have kept (and do keep) showing up for your child, and that is to be commended. I know full well that that continued showing up can get a little bit heavy and

13

a little bit discouraging, especially during difficult times or long stretches of wondering.

You have a full knowledge of your child's narrative, and I submit to you that the full knowledge of your child's narrative only serves to make their triumphs and their successes that much more beautiful to you. You understand *fully* them because you know the journey that it took to get there. Your heart gets enlarged in its breaking (and oh! the breaking it can undergo as a parent!), and that breaking makes space to hold a greater love and celebration during the good times.

No matter how much I love a child as their teacher, my heart will never be as big for them as their parents', because my heart will never break for them the to the same degree that a parent's will. I encourage you to recognize it as a privilege to sit in the parent corner of the triangle and to witness the *full story* of your child evolve.

I want to share some specific ideas with you that I learned first as a teacher and now try, every day, as a parent to implement in my own life. You can read this book cover to cover, or simply use it as a reference, flipping to the section or entry that seems best suited to your particular challenge (or challenges!) of the day.

Wherever you are in your journey, take heart in knowing that what you do matters, that joy can be found amid difficulty, and that this will help you grow.

SECTION 1

Parents & Teachers

Different Roles, Same Team

When my children began music studies at a very young age, I hesitated sharing the start of that journey with too many people, because I was afraid of being judged. Judged as being a fanatic, of pushing my kids into things *I* wanted them to do, of being a "Tiger Mom". But I've learned that that can happen to a parent no matter what she does, so I might as well bite the bullet and share.

For my younger daughter's third birthday, she received a cello. The tiniest, itty-bittiest lil' thing you've ever seen. She promptly named it Ariel, and christened the bow and case "Prince Erica" and "Ursula" respectively. I am her teacher, and she is my student. In the very beginning, when she was very young, we worked together every day, sometimes for up to an hour. During our practice sessions we would have temper tantrums (notice that I said "we" and not just "she"), and we would get frustrated, but we also had wonderful moments of love and discovery that happened along the way. The way we work together has evolved as her maturity and skill have too, but we still work together in a way that is meaningful and appropriate for our relationship and her skill level.

From that very first day, I kept in mind that this whole process was not about creating a cellist, but about creating a noble human being, and strengthening the bond between myself and my child.

My teaching philosophy says, "I believe children are strong, that they are capable, that they can learn to do anything and to do anything well with the right instruction and the right support. I believe that working through things that are difficult and take effort create a strong bond between parent and child and allow them to become closer. I believe that studying music cultivates character, discipline, empathy, understanding and appreciation for beautiful things; that it lifts us to a higher plane. I believe that experiencing the creative power of music allows children to feel these noble attributes and become noble people themselves. I believe that love is the greatest motivator and that, in the words of Dr. Suzuki, 'Where love is deep, much can be accomplished." Because I believe all these things, I teach music to children and their parents, to nurture them into becoming noble, strong, beautiful people."

It is easy to say those things as a teacher, but it's quite another to put them into practice as a parent, in the middle of the daily grind. My child was only 3! What was I thinking? You could argue that it was pointless to start a child in music lessons that young, as their pace of progress would be incredibly slow. That was true! (But is fast progress really more valuable than slow, personalized progress?) You could argue that it's what I wanted and not what she wanted, but do parents wait until their children show an "interest in reading" before they teach them to read? Or do they wait until they show a talent for "eating vegetables" before they serve them for dinner? No! Parents only learn about their children's talents and inclinations after they observe the children trying them out.

I also knew what music had done for my life, in teaching me to feel deeply, to serve and connect with others, and to feel close to God, or a higher power. And I wanted these things for my daughters, so I decided to make sure music was a part of their lives. I figured that the universe knew well enough that whatever children joined my family would get plenty of music, so it sent me my particular daughters, because they would benefit from it.

My cellist is my second and youngest child, and because of that I wondered when she was younger if she'd get enough attention from me. She's very easy-going and relaxed, which means she didn't always seem to need me. She's extremely self-aware and often sorts out her own problems and finds her own solutions. And while that was nice most of the time, the flip side was that I could see myself getting complacent, and not investing in our relationship, because its needs were not pressing.

I did want to make sure that I was investing enough in our relationship and not taking it for granted. I wanted to make sure I was really getting to know her, to connect with her, to love her. And I wanted to give her something special that uniquely bonded us together. So, I asked her one day if she'd like to learn to play the cello with me. She said yes, and that was all I needed.

Some days it wasn't easy, and many days it was excruciatingly difficult. But then there were *those* moments. The moments where I looked in to her face, my eyes level with hers because of the tiny chairs we were sitting on, and there was no one else in the room, or maybe even the world, but us. No phone calls, no friends, no sibling rivalry, no chores, no other obligations. Just her and me. I was learning how she learned. I was discovering what motivated her. I was celebrating her bright mind, her easy-going spirit, and her happiness. We were learning together how to work through difficult things. And I was cheering her on all the way. (Ok, sometimes I was sending her to time out and THEN cheering her on, but you get the idea.)

It was my hope as we started this journey that as we traveled to group classes and recitals and performances together, that we'd chat in the car about her life and her cares and her frustrations, that the journey to our events would be as enjoyable as the events themselves. It was my hope that working through this difficult yet rewarding process would bring us closer together, and teach us how to work through conflict. It was my hope that she would, in music as in life, support and complement her violinist sister, that there be no competition between them; only beautiful harmony. It was my hope that she would learn to feel love in a unique and powerful way. It was my hope that some day when I am gone, she would look back on the practicing and the struggle and the work and see a mother who cared deeply for her, who loved her so much that she gave her daughter something that would always connect the two of them together.

I remember before I became a music parent, when I was a teacher only. I would ask a student to do something at the lesson, and they would do it. And then we'd move on to the next item, I would offer correction, and an assignment, which the student would willingly accept and complete, and then we'd move on again. They were so cooperative! And because I saw them only once a week, the growth that took place between our meetings was observable and measurable.

Then when I became a music parent I'd work with my child at home. I'd ask my child to do an assignment or task, and the child would start crying, or would argue, or would become uncooperative. I witnessed as a parent all of the behavior I'd never seen as a teacher. The growth that happened every day was so gradual and infinitesimal, that I wondered if it was happening at all.

In short, as a parent my eyes were opened to a depth and nuance in the music-learning process that I could never have understood if I'd remained only a teacher.

I also learned, and learned well, that the parent is the limit that the child is testing. The teacher is the instructor and a source of guidance and wisdom, so the child rarely tests the teacher in the same way they test the parent. Learning this was both enlightening and frustrating for me. For one thing,

I immediately gained immense respect and empathy for all the music parents I'd ever worked with before. The fact that they kept their children coming to lessons, and that the children kept progressing in between lessons was now, to my eyes, some crazy sort of miracle! Additionally, this realization taught me that I had to take a different approach as a parent than I'd taken as a teacher. As a parent, I had to practice my relationship with my child as much as (or even more than!) we practiced the specific assignments given to us by a teacher. By making that small shift in my paradigm and treating my relationship with my child as *something to practice* opened up all sorts of possibilities for me. I hope it can for you too.

My cellist and I are eight years into this journey as I write this. And, miracle of miracles, I am seeing that hope of closeness, growth and love coming to fruition. My daughter is becoming a beautiful, capable, expressive cellist, and a confident, collaborative human being. Our relationship is deep, complex, and full of nuance and understanding because we have invested in its growth through our daily practice together. Can you, as you practice music with your child, practice your relationship with them too?

THE PRACTICE: Evaluating and Valuing Your Perspective

You, as the parent, know your child's journey better than anyone. Your understanding of his or her triumphs is sweeter because you know exactly what they had to go through to get there.

The following practice has two parts. You can do both, or only one. You can repeat this any time you are needing a little encouragement, or an insight into the greatness that lies within your child.

1. **The List**
   a. Make a list of the challenges you've seen your child overcome.
   b. Notice any patterns: How did they overcome? What did they learn from each one? What was their approach? How was resolution reached?

2. **The Letter**
   . Choose one challenge from this list and write your child a letter, expressing any of the following:
      i. Praise for overcoming the challenge
      ii. What you noticed about what they learned, or how they grew in the process
      iii. What you learned by watching them overcome
      iv. Your gratitude for learning through them

SECTION 2

Believe in Your Child's Capabilities

A Lesson in Space

For many years, my children and I have attended the local Suzuki Institute in our city. We always come away from the week inspired, rejuvenated and recommitted to our study of music. I also find that there are always so many layers of lessons to be learned that go far and beyond music study.

One such beautiful moment happened a few years ago in a masterclass with Helen Higa, a wonderfully sweet Japanese-American violin teacher from Hawaii. On my daughter's first day in the class, Helen asked her to play through the piece she had prepared for the class. As my daughter played through the first time, she arrived at a part in the music that had about four measures of rest, meaning she didn't play for about ten seconds. When my daughter arrived at that part, she put her violin in rest position and carefully counted those measures of rest. The silence in the room was almost oppressive. The mothers and other students in the room wondered what she was doing. I, as her mother who had practiced many months with her on this piece, knew she was being thoughtful and thorough; being careful not to rush through those important rests in the music. But I also wondered if the teacher would jump in and ask what she was doing. Would she think she had forgotten what came next, or would she simply say, "Go ahead and skip to your next entrance." But you know what Helen did?

She waited.

She could see in my daughter's manner that she was doing something with purpose. She stepped back and gave her the space she needed to complete the task in the way that was meaningful to her. She didn't interrupt, or hurry her on. She didn't dismiss lightly something that mattered to the student in front of her. She didn't assume that because she

27

was the teacher and the adult, that she knew better than the child. It didn't matter that we sat there in (slightly uncomfortable) silence for a solid ten seconds; she was willing to give my daughter the space she needed to be the person she is.

And you know what happened? My daughter just blossomed. Her confidence grew, she felt secure, and she gained an immeasurable amount of respect for that teacher who had stepped back and taken time to listen and understand instead of jumping in and telling her what to do.

Helen believed in the importance of giving my child space to explore, discern, understand, and develop her voice. Helen believed in the value of a child's perspective and experience. I came away that day in awe of the growth that happened right before my very eyes, when my child was allowed space in which to do all these things.

Can you guide your focus to giving your children space? Can you let them finish their thought before interrupting them and assuming you know what they mean? Can you give respect and deference to their experience which, while different from yours, is no less authentic?

Learning Tenor Clef

Equally as critical as giving our children space in which to discover and learn on their own, is the importance of standing by their side and supporting them when they are learning something difficult.

When I was about ten years old, I was given the assignment by my teacher to learn how to read tenor clef (a sort of "rite of passage" for any young cello student).

Though not a cellist, my dad was a musician and knew enough about this new skill to be my guide at home as I worked to develop it.

I cannot express to you the amount of frustration I felt trying to figure out how to read music this way. To me, it was akin to algebra (which also, when I first studied it, felt insurmountable and pointless).
I remember crying and crying because it was so frustrating. But through my frustration, my dad just stuck with me. He kept his cool, and didn't let my high emotions ignite his. Over and over he would say, "I know you can do this, try again. That's not the right note, try again." In that way, he stayed connected to me and, while not doing the task *for* me, helped see that the task could be done *by* me.

The interesting thing here is that I don't remember any specific notes he taught me, or any methods he used, or any specific pieces he taught me during that time. I actually don't remember *how* I learned this new skill.

But do you know what I *do* remember? I remember *being* with my dad. I remember the refining fire of learning something hard, and having someone by my side through the difficulty who deeply believed in my ability to master it. I remember us both in our pajamas, playing music together.

I remember thinking, "My dad believes in me. Maybe I really can do this."

I also remember noticing that my dad thought I was important enough to give me his time.

So I borrowed a bit of the confidence my dad had in me (when I was running short on my own) and somehow came out on the other side not only the master of a new skill, but full of the belief that I was worth spending time with.

I'm sure my dad had no idea the impact this experience would have on my life; he probably just thought he was helping me fulfill an assignment from my teacher for the week.

But that's the magic of this process: you never know what moments will carry with them the greatest lessons, the greatest impact.

And so it's worth it to keep trying, consistently and lovingly, so that when your child's heart is open or seeking or needful, your support and love are at the ready.

THE PRACTICE: Overlapping Strengths
1. **Write a list of your child's strengths**
2. **Write a list of your own strengths**
3. **Compare and contrast**
   a. Where do your strengths overlap with those of your child, and how can you combine them to make a united team?
   b. Where do your strengths differ? This shows you what you have to learn from each other. Can you guide your child graciously? Can you also *be guided by* your child graciously?

SECTION 3

Learning from the Teacher

Trusting the Teacher as a Guide

I remember when my oldest daughter began violin lessons. Her teacher seemed like some sort of powerful magician by the way she could both nurture my daughter while simultaneously demanding a high level of excellence from her. I wanted so badly to recreate that kind of positive, supportive, instructive environment for our home practice that I began to study exactly what the teacher was doing in lessons, and then I committed to implementing it at home.

If the teacher worked on scales for ninety percent of the lesson, then we worked on scales for ninety percent of the practice that week.
If the teacher heard every single review piece in a lesson, then we played every single review piece in every practice session that week.

If the teacher had my daughter drill measure 25 thirty times with the metronome at 60, then we did that very same thing every day in practice that week.

I found that as we diligently incorporated into our daily practice the work patterns set forth to us in weekly lessons, great progress happened. My daughter learned how to focus, how to drill, how to listen and discern, and how to work hard. It was not without bumps along the way! But by carefully repeating the patterns given to us in lessons, our practices became a laboratory for tremendous growth.

Practice makes patterns, after all.

Even though I myself was a musician and a music teacher, I decided to let my daughter's teacher be the expert. I trusted her years of experience, her wisdom, her optimism for my child's growth, and the understanding she had gained from working with hundreds of children and families over many, many years. When I decided to do this, to be the *support* to the teacher rather than trying to insert my own expertise in the way, I became free. And so too did my child.

This isn't to say my own skills and talents got left by the way side, but rather that I used them to *support*, rather than to *supersede,* what was being given to us.

This may have been the greatest challenge I faced as a music parent: to learn how to be a support to (not an architect of) my child and her teacher as they crafted their own working relationship. To learn how to suspend what I thought I knew about the whole thing, and instead, trust our teacher as a guide. To be open to learning and guidance, the same way I hope my child can learn to be.

And when my child saw, over time, that I trusted our teacher and was open to the guidance she had for us, rather than me thinking I had all the answers and knew better than our teacher, my child learned the same attitude and approach. Her openness to learning and willingness to trust the teacher deepened, and so too did her ability.

The Power of Positive Language

As I studied exactly what was done in lessons and then tried to model that in home practice sessions, I began to notice that not only was our teacher exact in her assignments, drills, and goals, she was also a master of language. In seven years of weekly lessons, and countless group classes and studio activities, I only ever heard this teacher use positive language. There was never a "no" or "not quite", or even anything with a shade of negativity to it.

When I first noticed this, I thought maybe it was a fluke of the week or the lesson. So I decided to begin writing down some of the phrases she used, just in the margins of the notebook page where I kept our assignments. To my amazement, I found that this pattern remained consistent throughout the entire time my daughter studied with her; seven full years! I have seven years' worth of notebooks filled with ways to use positive language to encourage discernment and growth!

What's more is that the language was always specific, positive, and personally-applicable, while still leaving room for growth. Here are just a few of my favorite phrases from those seven years:

- You have rhythm, I can feel it
- You're getting good at this
- That was real skill
- You saw something I didn't
- I think you found your sound
- Trust that you can do it
- Let me hear that you understand
- You've worked it out; thank you
- You get used to it by going slow
- That was purely sunshine
- You know every part of the bow

- The tone is changing
- Vivaldi would be so pleased
- I love that you have worked with a focused feel
- I'll eat that for breakfast!
- Tone is our goal, whatever we do
- You kept at it until you figured it out
- You can teach me
- This sounds like music now
- Wonderful work

Swimming in language like this for over an hour each week had a profound effect on myself and my daughter. I saw her insecurities melt away and give way to the desire to try, to seek, to exercise curiosity and to take risk, because she was in a safe place and could do so without any negative repercussions. I saw my inner critic dissolve and make way for a parent who could see the good in her child, and celebrate the extreme effort she was putting forth into the learning and mastering of a musical instrument.

It is so important for us to create an environment conducive to growth in our relationships and our homes. Language is one of the surest ways to manipulate and affect the energy and emotions in a room, and in a relationship. As you choose positive, clear, encouraging language in your dealings with your child, you will see a difference in your relationship.

In fact, I have outlawed the word "hard" in my own studio, and try desperately not to use it with my children in their music studies. I require students AND parents (and myself!) to replace it with something else, such as:

- That is interesting
- That will help me grow
- I'm learning to improve this
- I'm working on understanding this
- I need more information about…
- I'd like to develop…

It is remarkable what happens to a child when they are surrounded by positivity, and the idea that any stumbling block can really just be a stepping stone to more growth. This is different than minimizing or not acknowledging the difficulty. Rather, this approach creates a safe space in which a child can approach the difficulty with support, positivity, and curiosity.

THE PRACTICE: Building a Supportive Relationship with the Teacher

1. **Speak respectfully to and about the teacher**
   a. Notice how your child responds to their teacher when you talk in positive ways about them and the assignments they give you and your child.

2. **Keep a written record**
   .
   a. Take notes in lessons not only of what specific assignments you are asked to do, but also what encouraging, positive language your teacher uses when working with your child.
   b. Notice which phrases or approaches seem to be most helpful to your child, and begin to use them at home.

3. **Reach out**
   .
   a. Teachers have a lot on their plates! Contact your child's teacher and offer to help with something specific. Here are some ideas of things teachers often need help with:
      i. Printing programs for recitals
      ii. Bringing refreshments to studio events
      iii. Sending emails
      iv. Organizing events (such as chair set up at recitals, etc)
      v. Ask your teacher for specific ways you can help

SECTION 4

Choices Have Consequences

Taking Responsibility for the Life You Create

All choices have consequences. I'm sure you've had this discussion many times with your own children. Don't we all? If you go to bed late, you're going to be tired in the morning. If you eat only junk food, you're going to have a tummy ache. If you are kind to other children, you will find you have lots of friends.

It's important that we as parents recognize that our choices also have consequences.

If we choose to lose our temper during practice sessions, it's not going to be a good experience for those involved, and our child will be reluctant to work with us again. If we fail to follow through on the assignments given to us by our teacher, our child won't grow in the way they otherwise could have. If we choose to involve our children in many different activities, more than just music, that is ok! That choice simply means that that child's growth trajectory will be different than another child who focuses solely on one activity. *There's nothing wrong with this.* The difficulty comes when we compare our outcomes or our growth with families who have chosen a different path. It's so important for us as parents to take responsibility for the choices we make as we guide our children, and not get upset or discouraged when our results are different than someone else who has made different choices.

Throughout my years of teaching, I have had many occasions to hear parents bemoan the fact that their child is moving more slowly than one of their peers. Or that their child is somehow lacking compared to another child. We all know that comparing ourselves to others robs us of the joy we might otherwise have in our lives.

Someone who has encouraged their child to undertake music studies in order to enrich and better their life may be discouraged that the child isn't a virtuoso after just a short time of study. But if reaching a virtuoso's level of proficiency was never the original goal, why get discouraged if the child isn't a virtuoso when someone else is?

So often comparing our results to others' results pulls us off of our own journey; it derails us from our own values and the reason we began an undertaking in the first place.

What can keep us secure in our journey is realizing that we are the creators of our own lives. That means not only *refraining from comparing* our own path to someone else's, but also realizing that if things aren't working for us or our family, *we have the power within us to make a change.* Envision the outcome you wish to enjoy, and let yourself move toward it.

It takes courage to act upon this knowledge.
And living a life of intention is perhaps the most courageous thing we can do.

Getting Angry is a Waste of Time

A big choice we make as parents and families in this music education journey is how we deal with frustration and high emotions.

Dr. Suzuki once said, "Getting angry is a waste of time."

Or at least that's what I wrote down from the seminar I attended at the SAA conference in Minneapolis a few years ago. I'm not sure why the sentiment of that quote struck me with such force. It could be because I do have a temper. It could be because I am obsessed with using time wisely and efficiently.

It could be because I am often guilty of wasting my time and energy on getting angry. (I usually label it as "being passionate", so I sound like less of a terrible person.)

Lately I've been doing a lot of thinking about what it means to be a leader, to inspire people without compelling them. To nurture without forcing. To enable self-assessment and understanding without telling someone what to think or do. To acknowledge that it's completely alright that someone else's emotions and reactions might be different than mine.

I certainly don't have all the answers, but I am trying very hard to step back and let the people in my life have their own experiences without my judgement or commentary.

And one day, during practice with my 9-yr-old, I think I finally understood...
...at least a little bit more.

It had been a regular occurrence of late that my older daughter would throw a huge fit or tantrum at some point during her daily practice. Sometimes it was in the morning, sometimes the afternoon. Sometimes it was because she was tired or hungry, sometimes it was because she was frustrated learning new material. Sometimes it was because she was just having a day and feeling strong emotions.

Usually, it was a combination of these things.

I had found myself wondering why a bright, kind child who had played and practiced violin for 6 years would be in this situation. Aren't tantrums for 3-yr-olds? for beginners? Was I really such a poor parent that I hadn't yet figured out how to avoid this type of thing?

For the longest time, I felt like my role as her mother was to provide stability, security and boundaries. To be the thing that she could rely on, to be a steadying force in her life. To show her what was appropriate and acceptable, and what was not. To be her rock.

And then, she started to grow up. To think for herself. To have different ways of viewing things, or saying things. To have her own opinion. *(I cannot count the number of times she has retorted to me with the words, "In YOUR opinion", or "I'm sorry you heard it that way.")*

This strength is one of the things I love most about her!

But I was starting to see that my attempts to guide her were changing into attempts tocontrol or force her strength into my paradigm. And this was getting in the way of my relationship with my child.

Honestly, it hadn't been smooth sailing leading up to this day of difficult practice, and I'd found myself truly worrying about my relationship with her. It was under so much pressure that I was worried it would be irrevocably damaged.

Why couldn't she trust me? Why did she respond to me with such venom and anger sometimes? Why did she sometimes treat me with such disrespect and downright rudeness?

On the other hand, she could have been thinking those very same things about me. There are, after all, two sides to every story.

And suddenly that day, during practice, my understanding was expanded.

We came to the time for the tantrum, and instead of being the strong, secure, immovable strength in her life, I decided to let go. To not force her to feel one thing or the other. To not tell her that what she was feeling wasn't correct. To not heap consequences and time-outs on her because she wasn't behaving appropriately. To let go of what I thought she needed and listen to what she really was trying to say.

I simply let her sit on her chair and scream at me. Yell at me. Cry. Wail. Tell me why she didn't like this and that what I was doing was wrong and so mean. The force from that little child was hard to bear, she was so powerful.

But I didn't answer. I didn't comment. I didn't judge. Even in my mind. I just let the metronome tick away (which had been set earlier for a technique exercise) while my daughter berated me.

"Getting angry is a waste of time."

Could it be that instead of being her rock, I needed to be something else for her? Could I decide to be a soft place to land? Could I be the element in her life that enabled the dissipation of her strong emotions rather than tossing them back in her face, stronger than they were to begin with?

Could I change who I am because it is more important to love her than to be right?

Instead of replying in kind to my daughter's screams and anger, as had been usually the case, I simply let her emotions wash over me. She threw everything she had at me, and I let it pass right through me, like smoke rising from a fire.

And you know what, after a few minutes, the same thing happened for her. That passion, energy and frustration dissipated because I was not feeding the fire; I was her soft place to land, not a source of resistance. When it was clear that she was no longer held hostage by those feelings, I told her I loved her, and she replied in kind, her savage screaming being replaced by a more sincere, true voice. I told her it was ok to feel those strong emotions, and we remarked on how much better we felt after having let them go.

(I did this once. Could I be brave enough to do this again?)

She was such a sight, afterwards! Eyes puffy from crying. Her throat raw from screaming. But I choose to look at how hard she was trying, rather than how poorly she had behaved. Isn't she incredible? Isn't she strong? Isn't she amazing? Doesn't she deserve a soft place to land? Doesn't she deserve a better me?

Getting angry is a waste of time.

Aren't I privileged to get to be HER mother, to walk this journey with her? A child of spirit, strength, and determination?

Our practice that day ended with softness and connection, with truly seeing each other. Although more raw than when we had started, we were closer than when we had begun.

Maybe she'll remember those arpeggio fingerings and the new section in the Prokofiev. Maybe not. Maybe her tone or intonation improved by what we did that day. Maybe those scales and intervals make more sense.

But maybe not; and you know what? That's ok.

I'll tell you what had improved and what did make more sense after that day: how free I felt in letting go of my anger. How it would have been a waste of an entire afternoon to let those feelings stay in my heart. What had improved was my ability to change, to be soft, to stabilize, to validate, to truly see my child. To use that moment of high emotion as a chance for connection

I learned that day that to *love* is more important than any security and stability I could offer my children.

THE PRACTICE: Getting Clear On Your Motivations

1. **Write out a list of reasons why you enrolled your child in music lessons**
   a. This could include, but is not limited to
      i. Learning discipline
      ii. Strengthening parent/child relationships
      iii. Giving child a peer group
      iv. Giving child a way to serve
      v. Continuing a family tradition of music

2. **Ask yourself the following questions:**
   .
   a. Are my actions supporting the motivations for studying music in our family?
   b. If not, what needs to change?
   c. Am I short-changing my child's growth by comparing her to a peer? Or am I celebrating it by comparing herself to a past version of herself?
   d. Have my family's needs changed from when we began music study? Meaning, do we need to adjust our goals?

SECTION 5

The Importance of a Peer Group

Why I Didn't Quit, Even Though I Wanted To

When I was ten years old, I attended a Suzuki Institute in my home town and became connected with three other girls my age to form a string quartet. It was magic from the very beginning! We became best friends instantly and stayed together as a quartet all the way through high school, making music together until we all went away to college at different music schools across the country. These ladies are some of my very best friends to this day! We live in different corners of the country but it doesn't matter: we are connected by our love of music and our shared experiences.

As young music students (we called ourselves "The Quarter Notes"), we had so many adventures together! We rehearsed every Friday afternoon, and went from performing our very first gig (a birthday party for my 5th grade teacher's mother, where we were each paid $5 and a York peppermint patty) to performing for two different governors of Utah, the unveiling of the Salt Lake Olympic Logo, and even performing at Abravanel Hall as guests of some members of the Utah Symphony.

Besides our music studies, we spent time together just being ourselves. I remember many times in Junior High thinking to myself that if I could just get through the difficult week at school (with friends, or homework, or what have you) that I'd be able to see my music friends on Friday and all would be well. Because we were all working hard on our music, and learning at a young age what it means to really sacrifice for something and really cultivate discipline, there was a deep, unspoken level of understanding between us. There was no drama in our friendships, because there was no time for it. (Perhaps it was burned off by all our hours in the practice room).

Our friendship is what kept me going throughout those difficult teenage years, when I felt like my life was hard, and difficult, and unraveling around me. I knew that if I gave up my music studies, I would also be giving up my friendship and association with these wonderful ladies, and that wasn't something I was willing to do. Their friendship was my safe harbor in that difficult time of adolescence.

And let's just think about this too: The wonderful thing about nurturing a peer group for your child is that it also creates a peer group for you! As you're attending music activities with your child, you will meet other parents who are there too. Parents who have similar goals, similar ideals and similar struggles. These fellow parents can become valuable to you as inspiration, as motivation, and as *friends* in your own life.

Now that I have perspective on this as a parent, I look back on this beautiful part of my life and realize that it didn't just happen by itself. I was able to develop meaningful relationships with my Quarter Notes because my parents supported and facilitated experiences that would nurture those relationships and allow them to unfold naturally, gradually, organically, beautifully. They got me to rehearsals every Friday. They were willing to check me out of school early to go perform at various functions. They took turns driving us to our various performances before we could drive ourselves. They partnered with the other parents to make this magical experience happen for us. They made the financial sacrifices to send us to summer camps together. It took heavy lifting, and I recognize that. It truly is one of the greatest gifts my parents could have given me as a teenager: a safe space inhabited by kind, hard-working peers who loved and accepted me as I was, while pushing me to be better. Inhabiting this space as a teenager is what allowed me to feel free enough to find myself.

And because these girls anchored me during a time in my life where my sense of self was nebulous, and my mind and heart were full of questions, I was able to push through that period of doubting and come out the other side confident, brave, and committed to making music an important part of my life. I don't know where I would be today without them.

THE PRACTICE: Facilitating Peer Experiences

1. **This week, organize a group experience for your child and their music peers.** Ask yourself: what kinds of group experience would be beneficial for your family? What would fit in to your family goals, family schedule, etc?

   Here are some ideas that range from simple to complex. Don't feel like you have to do everything on the list! What matters is *facilitating connection* with the music families around you. Build your village, and then stand back and watch it build your child.

   - **Organize a practice play date.** Invite your child's friend over. Let them practice together for a set amount of time, and then put away the instruments and let them play · together!
   - **Invite friends to perform together in the community**. Farmer's markets, retirement facilities, churches, etc are great places for kids to get service/performing opportunities.
   - **Host a weekly music club.** A mother in my neighborhood did this when I was growing up and it was so much fun! Every Wednesday at 1 pm in the summer, the music club would meet at her home and each person would play one piece for the group. Afterwards we'd have treats and play time.
   - Invite friends from your studio to join you for **ice cream after a recital**.
   - **Offer to carpool** with a family in your studio.
   - **Bring notes of encouragement** or small gifts for the student who has a lesson before

or after your child each week. Leave these items in their case or by their shoes.

- **Host a parents' night.** Invite parents from your studio to gather and have refreshments as you discuss anything from parenting books to articles to Ted Talks. If it goes well, make it a regular occurrence.
- **Support the formation of a small performing group** for your child to participate in with regular rehearsals.
- Attend all studio group activities and classes regularly.

SECTION 6

The Best Practice is Consistent Practice

Gardens in Japan

I had the opportunity to travel to Japan with my family in the summer of 2017. It was a highlight of our lives. We remark often on that experience and all we learned and discovered there.

One thing I especially loved about Japan were the gardens and parks. Lush greenery, vibrant colors, flowers and trees as far as the eyes could see. And so beautifully manicured and cared for. It fills my soul just thinking about it.

I remember visiting a particular garden in Ueno Park in Tokyo. I looked around me, taking it all in; feeling my soul and heart expand at the beauty and life around me. As my eyes roamed the landscape, they landed on a small figure in the distance, carefully bent over a small shrub. After closer examination, I could see that it was a groundskeeper, painstakingly caring for his one small corner of the park. I approached to watch his careful work and was astonished to find that he was using the smallest shears I'd ever seen in a garden, clipping off a tiny leaf here, a small offshoot there. In my Western ignorance, I thought to myself, "Why use such small shears? You can't even tell if they are making a difference in the big picture. No one will know tomorrow that this shrub has been trimmed today."

My ignorance prevented me from making the connection between care and beauty.

The day I returned home to my neighborhood in the United States, I was met by a large truck outside my neighbor's front yard. A tree in the front had grown too large and then become so diseased to the point that it had to be torn down. A large staff of workers spent the better part of two days chopping down this tree, shredding it into chips, and trying to remove the stump from the ground. It was loud, arduous work that interrupted the neighborhood for days. When they were finally finished, their efforts left a gaping wound in my neighbor's front yard.

The contrast could not have been more stark. The message could not have been more clear.

I realized in that moment the wisdom of the Japanese groundskeeper and his use of small shears. Small, consistent, daily efforts of care not only help cultivate beautiful growth, they prevent against devastating wounds that result when we neglect those things we wish to nurture. Should we not also take the same approach to the study of music with our children? Can we commit to small, consistent daily efforts to care for them and help them cultivate their own beautiful growth?

One Foot In Front of the Other

I like to run. What started out as a way to lose some weight I gained during my first pregnancy has turned into this incredibly cathartic hobby for me which allows me to stay physically and mentally healthy. And I love that while running, the solitude, endorphins, fresh air, and quiet all mix together into this magical potion that allows my brain to discover insights that I may have otherwise missed.

A few weeks ago, I was running outside on a clear Friday morning. My husband was home with the girls and we were getting ready for a vacation, so I had all the time in the world. No deadlines to meet, no schedule to adhere to, no students to get back to. So, I let my mind wander.

And wander it did. Wandered back to a class I attended while at the Suzuki Association of the Americas Conference in Minneapolis back in 2010. The class was on Eurythmics, which is basically learning how to express rhythm through your body; the idea being that it must be corporeally understood first, before it can be correctly expressed on your instrument.

The presenter of the class, a remarkable cellist and teacher by the name of Jared Ballance, began the class by asking us what seemed like a simple question: How do you walk? What do you do to get from point A to point B?

Most of us blurted out the first answer that came to our minds: you place one foot in front of the other. Seems logical enough, doesn't it?

But that's wrong. Seriously. Try it. If you just stand there and put one foot in front of the other, you will go nowhere. (If you're shifting your body weight, you're cheating!) You will make motion and use energy, and you will make literally no progress.

The presenter went on to explain that you actually walk by shifting the weight in your *center*, in your *core*. As your center moves forward, your feet and legs walk and move in order to keep you from falling down. *The movement of your feet is not the impetus for motion, it is the result of motion.* Seriously. Try it. Stand up and lean forward. Your foot will automatically step out to keep you from falling on your face.

And, as I was running that day, I decided to apply this idea of moving from my core to my running. Instead of making sure one foot went in front of the other and that I was keeping a steady pace, I instead shifted my focus to my core, my very center, my heart. As I propelled it forward, the running became easier. I let my inward motivation and desire to move direct how I was moving. I was no longer focused on the motions, but rather on the direction and the end goal. As I took my attention off of my feet and legs and focused it into my center, I found I could move more quickly with less effort, and that I was actually enjoying the whole process. In fact, I even decided to run a longer route than I'd originally set out to do.

And then, since my longer route allowed for more time for introspection, I got thinking some more. What about my goals and my life? Do I get so focused on the motions, that I forget about my inner motivation for *doing* those motions? Do I get so focused on the *how* to get somewhere, that I don't let myself just move in that direction, trusting that my body or my soul or my heart will know how to take the next step and the next? Do I become weary because I'm focused down at my feet, rather than at the vision on the horizon? Am I so tired from moving, that I can't look up and enjoy the whole process?

You can spend your life trying to run by putting one foot in front of the other, but until you are moving from within, you will get nowhere. True progress is achieved not as a result of motion and action, but of an inner commitment to lean toward and then arrive at a certain destination. The things you do with your life are a result of the route your heart is dictating.

So, next time you're in the middle of working towards a goal, take your attention off of your feet, and instead just let your center move towards your goal. You'll find yourself less weary and more likely to enjoy the journey.

"There's No Substitution for Repetition"

In my teaching studio, there is a sign hanging on the wall that says, "There is no substitution for repetition." Over time, this has become one of my teaching mantras, and perhaps the most important one. I explain to my students that it is not enough to *know* something; in order to master it you must *do* it. And do it again. And again! It is only through correct repetitions that we begin to master our craft. There is no shortcut to becoming proficient, no easy way!

I touch on this concept daily with all my students, and even the youngest ones can explain to you what that sign on my wall means.

One day, I ran into the mother of one of my students who was in second grade at the time. She told me that he had just started soccer that week, and when she had picked him up from his first practice, she had asked him how it had gone. What did you do? What's your team like? Did you like it? What did you learn?

He explained to her that as the coach asked them to do some drills, some of the team members began to complain about how boring the drills were, and how many times they'd been asked to do them.

"So," explained this 8-yr-old student to his mother, in a matter-of-fact tone, "I just told them that 'there's no substitution for repetition.' "

This student had articulated to his soccer teammates what he'd learned through music study: that it is not enough to *know*, we must take what we know and then *do* it.

Only by doing, does a skill move from our mind into our heart, and from our heart into our understanding.

This is true not only for practicing skills on our instruments, but also for any skill we wish to develop: be it patience, perseverance, diligence, or consistency. It is by *trying* the skill, not just thinking about or committing to the skill, that we can become masters of it.

THE PRACTICE: Developing Consistency

1. **Practice 100 days in a row with your child.** You get to decide:
   a. Whether or not there is a time requirement to make a practice session count
   b. Whether there is a reward at the end (I strongly recommend going out for ice cream!)
   c. Whether you get extra credit for cooperative or peaceful practices
2. **See what happens** after you have completed the 100 days. Your troubles will not all be behind you, but you will find that they are more manageable because they are being addressed on a consistent, careful basis. Your persistence will have grown into habit, your habit into ability, your ability into understanding.

SECTION 7

**Recognizing and Valuing
Your Child's Experience**

"I Put the Shoes on All By The Self"

One day when my oldest daughter was three years old, she refused to put her socks on when I asked her to. So, when I counted the proverbial "1...2...3..." and she still didn't have them on, I put them on her myself. I was still young in my parenting, and was focused so much on *doing the right thing*, in order to *get the right result.*

Additionally, it was important to me as a mother to follow through with what I had told my children I would do. I wanted them to be able to depend on me. I wanted to teach them respect and discipline. I wanted to be the guide that helped mold them into individuals with good character. I wanted to provide security, foundation, and dependability. And I was going to do my best at meeting all of these goals and standards at all times, even when it came to the putting on of socks.

It would be an understatement to say that weeping and wailing and gnashing of teeth then began to ensue. Screaming, swatting at me, and yelling at the top of her lungs, "I WANTED TO PUT MY SOCKS ON!!" My daughter was not about to let me get away with what I had just done.

What I had seen as an opportunity to teach her about correct behavior and doing the right thing and reaping consequences and yada yada yada, she saw as an infringement on her autonomy, on her chance to try it out on her own.

My initial reaction was to march her directly to a time out. You know, teach her discipline and boundaries, right? No one, under any circumstances, should be allowed to react that way, let alone to their mother. I was the parent after all! Wasn't it up to me to teach discipline, to enforce correct behavior, to instill respect and cooperation? Wasn't my perspective, with more experience and time behind it, more correct than hers?

Somehow, that approach didn't sit right with me that day. Somehow I tuned into my heart as it was telling me that just doing the right thing and getting those darned socks on my child's feet was not the most important thing going on right then. Somehow, I felt and then listened to a small, internal nudge that urged me take a breath, take a step back and look at it from my daughter's perspective. Somehow I could see past the desired outcome and into my child's heart in the present moment.

When I did that, what I saw astonished me. I somehow understood that the end result of getting the socks on was not as important as the process of learning how to do it herself. I saw that by diving in and doing it for her, not only did I rob her of the chance to practice and improve a skill, I was sending her a message that *I didn't believe she was capable*, and that she couldn't be trusted to do something herself, even though in reality she truly was more than competent enough to complete the task.

So instead of resulting to a time out or some kind of negative consequence, I took a deep breath and somehow found in me the patience and courage to wrap my arms around her and hold her in a firm but gentle hug. Instead of justifying my actions with ideas about respect and discipline and appropriate behavior, I just whispered in her ear, "I love you, Della."

And almost immediately, the tension and rage that had filled her little body completely dissipated, leaving in its place a happy, cooperative, secure child. A child who could relax because she had genuinely felt seen, and knew she was in a safe place.

That experience left me forever changed as a parent. I still knew I had a responsibility to guide and direct my child, to offer wisdom and teaching and council and protection as needed. But that day I learned that her experience and viewpoint are just as valid as my own; for together, our differing viewpoints and experience bring balance to our relationship. When I place too much importance on my own viewpoint and experience, our relationship topples out of balance.

I learned to ask myself not only what the end goal was, but what also was happening, from her perspective, on the way *to* completion of the goal. I started to ask myself: could I possibly do a better job supporting her growth on that path, rather than compelling her to the end result?

Wouldn't I want her perspective to be filled with wonder and confidence, rather than just always rushing to the end goal?

Isn't curiosity as valualble as completism?

Any parent will tell you that it's a fine line to walk, and I agree. It's a line I feel like I walk every day. But just knowing that my viewpoint isn't the only one, knowing that my child's experience is as valid as my own, has created space in my heart for balance and understanding that wouldn't be there if I had continued to take my dictatorial approach.

Valuable Lessons From
My (Then) Three-Year-Old

This selection was written many years ago, shortly after my oldest daughter began her violin lessons. I leave it in this book as it was originally written, to illustrate the rawness I was feeling during that magical, sacred time of beginning a new journey with my child.

I recently took on the role of Suzuki parent, as my three-year-old daughter began violin lessons a few months ago. I figured that my experience as a Suzuki student and Suzuki teacher would have perfectly prepared me for this experience in that third corner of the Suzuki Triangle: that of Suzuki parent. But I've learned that it certainly isn't as cut and dry as I thought it would be. Fortunately, my daughter has taught me some pretty powerful practice lessons.

The power of rewards

Children can accomplish a great deal with the right motivation. The trick is to find what works for your child. The night following every lesson, the Practice Fairies arrive at our house. During the night, they leave out new practice treats for the week and one "large" reward for my daughter. Earning this large reward was originally tied to an expectation: if she completed some big practice goal for the week then she earned the reward. But I soon found that that was too much pressure for this particular child. So, the fairies gradually switched their approach. Instead of bringing a prize that my child could earn for a certain goal, they simply left her a gift of love. The giving of the prize came to say, "I see how hard you have been working. I recognize your effort. I love you for trying, even when it's hard to try." This change from rewarding accomplished *tasks* to rewarding the *character trait of perseverance* made a huge change in our practice sessions for the better. It became about doing your best and doing it consistently, rather than meeting some external measurement.

We are capable of exactly what we think we are capable of

How many of us have heard the words that whether you think you can or you think you can't, you are right? The same is true when it comes to working with our children. If we focus on their limitations or their shortcomings or their struggles, that is all we see and that is what they begin to see. But when we focus on their progress and their capabilities, these things expand. I make it a point to record the positive comments my daughter's teacher gives her in her lessons. When I open that notebook to practice at home and I see words like, "This sounds wonderful!" or "What a beautiful sound!" or "This is showing lots of progress" then my confidence in my daughter grows, and I am given the strength and faith necessary to tackle another week of practicing. And she can feel that.

Another lesson my daughter has taught me is that practicing is about developing my relationship with my child, not only about helping her progress as a musician. There are plenty of days I get ready to practice and find myself thinking, "Oh boy, here we go again. Do I have the strength to get through another day of 100 tukkas? I'm not sure I can take the monotony of another practice session." It's easy to look at it as just a chore to be done, to check off of a list. But then I remind myself that, in this day and age of busy and demanding schedules, with families running in every direction, it is a privilege to be able to spend focused one-on-one time *every day* with my child. Every day I get to sit down at her level, look her in the eyes, watch her progress step by step, see her eyes light up when she accomplishes something. Every day! When I remember that, it becomes less of a chore and more of a privilege.

And the most important thing I've learned (so far) is that this isn't about me, it is about my child. We have certainly had our struggles in learning how to work together. Not every practice session has been flowers and puppies and "I love yous". But I learned early on that whatever I thought I knew about this process, I only knew *from my own experience in this process*. The greatest difficulty I have had has been in removing my ego and my agenda and my understanding and looking at things purely from my daughter's point of view. I have probably played Twinkle ten thousand times, but she has not. So of course, I have it memorized, but she is still learning how. If she makes a mistake, it is evidence of her growth, of her trying, of her taking those first few precious steps on her own. And the amazing thing is that when *my* pride and ego are removed, we actually *do* have "I love yous" and smiles and bright eyes in practice sessions.

Simply being open to learning from and with your child can make all the difference.

Practice Fairies: Applying Practical Magic to Practice Sessions

Speaking of the Practice Fairies, I often get asked about the darling little helpers that come to our house weekly. Read on if you'd like to know in detail how they actually function at our house. The ideas here are my own, and I freely share them, in the hopes that it will make another child's (or parent's!) musical journey more beautiful.

My oldest daughter began playing the violin at the age of three. At that time, fairies and imagination and play were our *life*. And I loved it. Many days, my daughter insisted on wearing her fanciest dress up with coordinating tiara for practice. (I can still see her in my mind's eye: pink tutu, rainbow crown, curly hair. So cute!)

This particular daughter is also an interesting combination of strong and fragile. I knew she was capable of greatness, and when she focuses, there is no stopping her! But through working with her, I had also discovered that any kind of external pressure would just make her wilt. And so, the idea of the fairies (who could act as a buffer between my intensity and my daughter's tenderness) was born. It was so successful, that I continued the tradition when my younger daughter began her own music journey as a tiny, 3-yr-old cellist.

The gist of it is this: the night after lessons, the Practice Fairies come and bring each of my daughters a new set of practice cards. The cards contain various exercises/drills/review pieces/tasks to be performed during practice, all taken from the most recent lesson. Along with the cards, the fairies leave some kind of treat for the week. Usually it's something small: a sheet of stickers, a package of smarties, a new pencil, etc. Some weeks it's really big, like a new dress or even a trip to Disneyland

(which only happened once; and after many months of planning and saving at that. Still, it was the *best* surprise.)

Over time, the cards have evolved. At first, it was simply a handful of simple exercises. But the number of cards and their complexity have grown as we have progressed along our journey.

The year my oldest entered first grade, which meant she was now in school all day, we had to get creative and efficient with the way we used our time. At that point, the practice cards evolved to consist of the following three categories:

1. <u>Green cards:</u> These were cards she did before school in the morning with her dad (while I was teaching). These included things she had a good handle on, and that her dad, who did not regularly attend lessons and therefore didn't have the full picture of the teachers' instructions in mind, could help her with. This included review pieces, note reading, and some simple exercises.

2. Pink cards: These are cards she did with me immediately upon her return home from school, after a snack and some relaxing time. These cards were the most complex in nature, and made up the bulk of our practice. They included new pieces, new concepts, and polishing pieces: things that I felt she needed guidance from me on, since I was the parent who was regularly present at the lessons and could help remember specific instructions from the teacher.

3. Yellow cards: These were cards that I let my daughter do by herself. A few of them were simple exercises that she did every day (and had done every day for many years). I did occasionally check on these, to ensure that correct habits were being strengthened. But it was also a chance to allow my child to take responsibility for some of her practice. The yellow cards also included a few "fun cards":

items that break up the practice. "Fun cards" switched out weekly and could include such things as hug card, call dad, do a cartwheel, take a drink, etc.

Some cards were actually books: a set of cards stapled together in a certain order. For example, my children each had a "bow book", which was a set of cards containing bow exercises that were stapled together. Each card in the bow book had written on it a specific bow exercise. These bow exercises had to always be done in the same order, and so that's why they were stapled together in a book, in an unchanging sequence. Once the child finished an exercise, they turned a page, like in a story book, and did the next exercise on the next page.

If we were short on time, then we did what we could. For example, if my child didn't finish all the green cards in the morning, then she put the undone cards in a baggy and started with those the next day. We didn't try to cram green cards into the afternoon during time that is set aside for the pink and yellow cards. Likewise, if we had a busy afternoon, then we cut out the yellow cards, making sure we did them the following day. Pink cards were sacred! They were done every day.

My younger daughter, who studies cello with me, was only in school two days a week at this time so we had no need for a color-coded system. We had at our disposal that most sacred of all resources: time! I just made sure her cards matched her needs, and that the fun cards rotated weekly.

My daughters were allowed to choose what order they pulled the practice cards out of the bowl, so they had a sense of variety and ownership (which are crucial to keeping up a child's interest and endurance!) Prizes were also earned weekly regardless of the quality and quantity of practice. Making the reward contingent upon the performance put too much pressure on a young student. I believe that at that young age, they should be rewarded *simply for trying*, for doing their best, for sticking with it day after day. Consistent striving is what matters: THAT is when progress is made.

We have already passed the day that we outgrew the fairies at our house. Fun Cards and treats and trips to Disneyland have been replaced by my daughters taking responsibility for their own practice. This is as it should be. It was my privilege to guide them and train them as they found their own way, to teach them to fly and then to step back and watch them soar. That is what the Fairies helped me to do. What made this venture successful for me was marrying my approach as a disciplined, organized, hard-working parent with the ideas and views and needs of my daughters: fairies and fun and imagination! It was a combination that served us well for many years.

Fairies might not be the right approach for your family, but that's now what it's about. What it really comes down to is the realization that this journey in music *belongs to your child*, more than it does to you. So tailor that journey to them. Find what inspires them. Find what motivates them. Maybe it's not fairies. Maybe it's gnomes, or charts they can fill out, or big challenges, or goals they can work towards. The fairies worked for us for many years, but they didn't work for us forever, and they won't work for everyone. But that's ok. Isn't constant evolution part of parenthood?

Taking the time to find out what inspires and motivates your child is one of the most amazing privileges of parenthood. Make the effort to find this, and you will also find magic along the way.

Practice Fairies Unveiled

For five glorious years, my daughters looked forward to weekly visits from the Practice Fairies, who brought them notes, treats, toys and goodies in addition to new practice assignments for the week. These little helpers were a buffer between my driven personality and my young daughters' tenderness. They taught me how to reward my children's effort, not just their results. They guided me in making clear, practical assignments for daily practice. They were a source of wonder and love in my family's life. They took us from Twinkle Little Star to the Bach Double Violin Concerto.

And then one day, after five years of magic, my cellist asked me point blank, "Mom, are you the Practice Fairies?"

I felt my stomach drop to the floor. You see, I am committed to honesty with my children in all things, and though the easy thing would be to continue to perpetuate the myth and the magic, I also knew that I would be more true to who I am as a parent and person if I had a direct conversation.

So I replied by asking, "What do you think?"

And our conversation continued as follows:

Della: "I think you are"
Aliya: "I'm not sure"

Me: "How would you feel if I were the practice fairies?"

Aliya, getting teary-eyed but smiling bravely: "A little bit sad"
Della, smiling with a mix of triumph and disappointment: "Grown-up"

And so, I told them the truth.

"I am the Practice Fairies. And over the years, I made all those cards and left all those surprises because I love you. And, just because I don't have wings, am not invisible, and cannot do magic tricks, doesn't mean I can't still be a Practice Fairy, right?"

To which they bravely smiled, laughed through their tears, and assured me that yes, I could still be a Practice Fairy.

I told them that I had carefully prepared the practice cards every Thursday night for almost five years.
I told them that their dad and I had saved up our money to finance that trip to Disneyland that the fairies had brought them.
I told them that I was the one who chose the matching earrings, those black dresses, the Else & Anna dolls, and countless other little prizes.
I told them I had read and collected and saved the notes they had so lovingly written to their fairies, and that those notes are and always will be precious to me.

I pulled back the curtain, like the Wizard of Oz, to show them that this magical portion of their life had been orchestrated by me, to fill their lives with wonder and goodness and love.

And then we all cried a little.
Cried at the realization that a little bit of magic would forever be only a memory in their lives.
Cried that the memories of the fairies' visits would always look a little different now.
Cried to realize that these years of wonder and imagination and magic were slowly starting to fade into the past.

As I tucked them into bed that night, Della said, "I'm a little disappointed to know that you that you are the Practice Fairies."

To which I replied, "It's ok to feel disappointed, it's like a little bit of the magic is gone, isn't it?"

"Yeah," she said. "But at least we know you're not Santa Claus, right?? Because, like, how would you be able to give presents to all the children in the whole world on just one night, right?"

"Yeah...right..." I softly replied, as I hugged her goodnight, maybe a little more tenderly than usual.

For all my value on honesty, I just couldn't do it twice in one day.

And then I spent the next hour crafting practice cards and surprises to leave for my daughters.
Because it was Thursday night, after all, and the Practice Fairies were due for a visit.

Glass Half Empty or Half Full?

So often in our lives, we are led to believe that there is only one correct perspective; only one right way to do a thing, or one right emotion to feel about a thing. But can that really be true? Is everything either/or, or could it be that there are as many ways to think and feel about, and then do, a particular task that's in front of us as there are people who are up to that task?

One night at dinner, my husband mentioned the idiom of the "glass being half empty or half full." Our girls hadn't ever heard of it, so he explained it to them.

And that started an engaging conversation about how each of us would view a glass of water. This is what we determined when we asked each other how we felt about a glass filled with some amount of water.

Is the glass half full or half empty?

My husband: The water in that glass could be used for so many things! You could use it to wash dishes, or to water the garden, or to brush your teeth, or to make lemonade. There are so many possibilities for that water! Think of all you could do with it!

Younger daughter: There is enough water in the glass to share with five people. I will find five more glasses and divide the water evenly so we all have enough. I love sharing with people! That water is a way to bring people together!

Older daughter: That water is special and beautiful and valuable. It should be saved and savored. I will set it on a shelf in my room and keep it safe. I will feel secure knowing it is there and not being wasted or used up. I won't need to look at it or spend time with it or use it. I know I have stored it safely and that is sufficient.

Myself: There's water in the glass; no need to philosophize about it. Let's move on to our next task.

We laughed and laughed at the range of views and opinions about that glass of water!
And then we asked ourselves, is one opinion better than the others? Or is it possible that each view is valid? Is it possible to take this viewpoint and that viewpoint and have them work together in a way that benefits all?

When you are struggling while working with your child, ask yourselves how you feel about a glass of water, and see what it teaches you about each other.

What's Your Core?

I had occasion one day to talk with a friend of mine about the ups and downs of parenting; how you are always filled with *The Tug*. You know, that pull you feel when you are trying to balance two things?

You want to protect your children, but let them experience life.
You want to teach them discipline, but you want to show them unconditional love.
You want to give them opportunities, but allow them to learn to work.
You want them to make and have friends, but learn to stand on their own.

What a dance!

Sometimes the pulls from opposing sides are enough to feel like you're about to tear apart. And this is the space we inhabit almost daily as parents.

Then this friend said something to me that made me wake up, sit up, and take notice. She began describing her son's *core*. She listed all of these beautiful, positive, wonderful talents and attributes that she could see in him. At the time, he was only three, so to the casual observer he may just be a little boy. But to his mom, who knows him and loves him and sees him day in and day out, he is so much more. He is his Eternal Self, just in a little shell. It is completely possible, in fact probable, that a parent can know their child's depth when the child is young, even before the child realizes his depth himself.

My friend made the off-hand comment that because she sees so much good in her son, she's just hoping that as his mother she can ensure those things don't get lost. She valued his inherent worth enough that she sought to nurture and develop the good that is already there, rather than super-imposing her own ideas on him.

We spend so much time and thought and energy as parents teaching and training our kids; trying to change them. We try to change the way they sleep, what they eat, what they wear, where they go to school, who their teachers are, how they treat their siblings. And in our desire to teach and train, sometimes we cross the line and begin to *control*; to try to get them to be and do what we think they should.

Sometimes in our efforts to teach them correct behaviors, we incorrectly begin to try to *change who they are.*

This whole discussion with my friend made me think: why should I spend my parenting energy on trying to change my children?
Shouldn't I spend my energy just discovering their core? And loving it? And protecting and nurturing it, so that their unique and special gifts and talents can be fostered and grown and allowed to shape this world? Shouldn't I give credence to their way of seeing and doing things?

I have a daughter who is naturally out-going and fun-loving; who is a friend to everyone around her; who is nonplussed by bullies or change or problems; who can go with the flow and sing her way through it, all while inviting others to join in the dance with her.

I have another daughter who is tender and sensitive, and easily affected by the moods of those around her. She is sometimes distant, and alone, and can take a great deal of coaxing and emotional care.

I have sometimes, mistakenly, tried to mold my sensitive daughter into her fun-loving sister. But this does them both a great disservice, in valuing one's gifts over the other's.

From one I learn to dance and laugh and sing, from the other I learn to slow down and see depth and beauty and true empathy towards another.

What a mistake to try to change one into the other!

Yes, it's true: we all grow and change with age and experience. I certainly hope that I have grown in wisdom and understanding and capabilities now that I've been around the block once or twice. I have kicked bad habits and created new ones in their place. And I still have plenty of growth ahead of me.

But I also rejoice that my *core* is as it always has been: that I am fun-loving, that I enjoy a good pun, and a good challenge. That I relate to others and can feel their heartache, so I know how to reach out and succor them. That I am deeply moved by music and all things spiritual. That I have a deep and abiding belief in God and His goodness. This is my CORE, and I hope that it will never change. In fact, I would vehemently fight anyone who would *try* to change it.

So, can I not extend the same consideration to my children? Look at their cores not as a mix of strengths to be celebrated and weaknesses to be corrected, but as a uniquely lovely combination of traits that make them who they are, that allow them to experience this world in the way that is best for them?

When I approach my parenting this way, I begin to feel less anxiety and pressure about the "training" of my children, and instead learn to celebrate the growth, a strikingly beautiful and vibrant growth, that takes place when I step back and let them blossom as they were meant to blossom.

They are God's greatest gift to me, why would I ever want to change them?

THE PRACTICE:
Seeing Through Your Child's Eyes

1. **Away from the instrument, and NOT during a practice session, ask your child any of the following questions:**
    a. What do you enjoy about music?
    b. What do you enjoy about your instrument?
    c. What do you find challenging about learning music?
    d. What can I do to help you with these challenges?

2. **Reflect.**
    Were these answers what you expected? Or did you learn something new about your child and their experience through this conversation?
    Write down what you learned and how you felt about it.

SECTION 8

Growth Comes Through Struggle

How I Know

Parenthood is multifaceted, isn't it? One moment you're full of bliss and love at these little darlings around your feet, and the next minute you're screaming inside for some sanity and some peace and quiet. You crave alone time, and then feel guilty when you get it. When a child joins your life, everything about your world turns upside-down and inside-out, and you're somehow expected to keep on moving, like everything is normal, when in reality you're undergoing a most acute transformation, by learning what it means to *truly* love unconditionally. People all around you say, "Enjoy these days while they are little, enjoy the kiddos while they are young, while they still want to be home, while they are at your feet to mold and guide and love and be loved. Hold on to the moments, because they are so fleeting."

But sometimes it's hard to do that, because raising children takes monumental strength, patience and courage.

One of the ways I have come to make sense of this process is through writing, and I'm sharing much of that with you in this book. In my writing, I just wanted to capture these magical days of my children's childhood before they are gone, because they move along so quickly and can so easily get lost in the hustle and bustle of daily life. I know that next year, next month, even next week, my children will be different people because of what they've experienced and how they've grown. And I don't want to miss any part of this amazing process of them (well, *us*, really) growing up.

You may wonder how I, a mother of children who are still young, could possibly know that? How could I understand the value of the moment? How do I know just how fleeting these days are? How do I know to take time and put things aside and just be present with my daughters? How do I already know the heartache of them growing up, even though they are still young?

Feelings like this are more apt to be expressed by someone with much more experience behind them, and therefore wisdom within them; maybe a mother of the bride, or perhaps a first-time grandmother. How is it that these feelings have found their way into my heart before my oldest is even in high school?

Well, friends, this is why:

The reason I know these things is because one day I had a friend, and the next day she was gone. It's because one day this example of kindness and enthusiasm and laughter and love was only a phone call away, and the next day I was making arrangements to travel to her funeral. It's because in the weeks preceding her death, I ignored the nagging feeling to contact her, thinking oh I'll get around to it, and then I never did. And never could. I don't live in regret of this, because she wouldn't want me to. But I do let it remind me every day to take time to enjoy, to feel the beauty of investing in loving relationships, especially with my children.

Yes, my friend's too-short life taught me many things, but perhaps the thing about which I am the most grateful is that, by leaving, she taught me to love *in the moment*, to experience it, to say it, to share it, and to *feel* it, and to never put off expressing what you feel for even one minute, because you never know when circumstances may dictate that you wait a lifetime to share what you thought you could say just any old time.

You had yesterday with your children, and you will likely have many tomorrows with them too. But, the only thing we can feel and experience with them is the present. Are you here with your child, NOW?

Twinkle, Twinkle My Little Stars

I am not one to sugar coat the truth. My experience as a Suzuki parent has been full of raw, tough, strengthening lessons. I love what I'm learning with my children. But it is a lot of work.

And a lot of time. And a lot of joy and tears and frustration and triumphs and epiphanies and happiness and giggles and scratchy sounds and wrong notes....and now and then, I've experienced a moment of just all-consuming *awe*.

Because we are still on the Suzuki path after nine years of doing it, and because I'm a teacher and have seen many families come and go over the years, I'm often asked how to make it happen, and how to do it successfully. Some common questions are:

- how do you find time to practice?
- how do you get your kids to practice?
- how do you get them to listen to you?
- how do you get them to follow directions?
- In short, *how do you do it?*

The answers are threefold, and are very simple.

<u>We do it, because we make time for it.</u> We do not do play dates in the morning. We do not go out before lunch. We do not watch movies or play or go outside or visit friends or do anything until the practicing is done. If we go on vacation, the instruments come with us. If we know it's going to be a busy day, then we wake up early and get practicing done before we have to leave. What I've found in my journey is that making a set time for practice not only ensures that it will happen, but it reduces the amount of time arguing over whether or not it will happen. I have found in my years both as a parent myself and by observing other successful music families, that practice is generally

more successful if done first thing in the day. And the thing is, when practice is done first, play time is that much more magical and special, because it's not just taken for granted. I rarely hear my daughters ever say to me that they're bored (they know that if they say that, my suggestion is for them to get out their instruments and do some more practice!)

My daughters are able to progress, because we realize that there is no shortcut to success. A favorite saying in our house (ok, *my* favorite saying in our house) is "There's no substitution for repetition." This means that if you want to get good at something, just keep doing it. What an important thing for a child to learn! Nothing is hard; it is only unfamiliar. "Just try," we say over and over. And so the girls do, and so they progress and learn to not fear mistakes, but to view them as a step in the right direction. The actual task does not become easier with the trying; rather, it is our capacity to do that task which is increased. So, just try again!

We do it, because we are learning more than music. Oh, I could site studies about discipline and math skills and communication and success at school and language acquisition and all kinds of things that a child gains through music study, and I'm glad we're reaping those benefits. But I'm talking about something *much more personal* here. I am studying, for hours every day, just exactly *who my daughters are.* I have learned so much about them (and myself!) as individuals through this process. I am learning what motivates and what *moves* them. I gain a window into their soul and their minds and their understanding that no other process has been able to give me. I am sitting down every day for hours at a time, one-on-one with each of my children. I am at their level, looking them in the eye, giving them undivided attention, showing them that nothing else is more important to me at that moment than they are. What a powerful lesson for a child to learn from their parent: *You are important to me.*

The long and short of it is that practicing and studying music are not about getting my children to listen to *me*, to get them to do what *I* want. It is about giving them a beautiful vehicle with which to discover, and then to express, themselves. It's about developing and deepening and enriching our relationships. What I find along the way continues to surprise and inspire and amaze me. But those discoveries only happen if I abandon my agenda, my pride, my I-know-more-because-I'm-your-mom attitude, and make room for the magic my children are capable of.

Please don't think that everything goes swimmingly at my house all the time. That is not true. But I try to do my best, just as I require of my daughters. And we all commit to try better next time if the present attempt may have proved less than successful. I don't pretend to have all the answers for all situations and all children/parent combinations everywhere.

But I do know one pretty powerful answer. And that is to LOVE your child. I don't mean simply feeling affection for them. I mean opening up a place in your heart that is free from the influence of your pride and your will and your want to control, and reserve that soft, non-judgmental place *just for that child.* Remember that their experience is just that: their own, and not yours.

Love them by letting them make mistakes, and try again.
Love them by setting a high standard for them, and truly believing in your heart they are capable of it.
Love them by giving them your time.
Love them by allowing them to develop skills they can be proud of, and which they can share.
Love them by realizing that they are not you, *and that is ok.*

Love them by guiding them step by step along the way, and then letting go to watch them walk out on their own.

Love truly is the greatest motivator.

So twinkle on, my little stars.

THE PRACTICE: A Mantra

1. **Repeat this mantra to yourself during difficult times:**
   - ○ Growth comes from struggle
   - ○ I'm struggling, so I am growing
   - ○ I recognize the growth that is coming to my child through his/her struggle
   - ○ I love my child enough to embrace my own growth

SECTION 9

Change: The Only Consistency

Adapt

If there's anything I've learned in my years as a teacher and parent, it's that the only consistent thing in a child's life is the fact that they will grow. Through this growth they will change and be, quite literally, a new person (and yet, paradoxically, the same person) every day. Because their growth is *always* happening (even if the *rate* of it is not consistent), that requires us to continually adapt in the way we nurture, guide and care for them.

You know this from your own experience!

Just when you'd found a comfortable routine for nap schedules, eating times, food preferences, school schedules, family schedules, practice regimens, etc, your child hit a growth spurt, or developed a food allergy, or had problems at school, or experienced a change in family needs that tossed it all up in the air and required you to start over. Sometimes from scratch.

This need to adapt used to really rattle me. I am a person of structure and predictability. I need that for security! I could not be bothered to reinvent the wheel! My wheels were functioning just fine, thank you very much!

Until they were not.

What helped open my heart was when I learned that the *principles* behind my actions could remain true and unchanging, even while my *implementation of those principles* adapted according to my child's needs. In other words, I learned to focus on the <u>motion and direction of my wheels</u>, rather than the structure of the wheels themselves.

I began to ask myself what purpose my routines were serving, and then see if there was a way to implement that purpose in a new way that adapted to my child's needs. This paradigm shift guided me in successfully adapting nap schedules, school schedules, food allergies, problems at school, and needs in relationships.

When we base our actions on principles and then infuse those actions with love, we will find success.

So if you have found yourself in the middle of a routine that is working perfectly smoothly and beautifully and you have no bumps in the road, enjoy it! Because you know you will have to adapt soon enough!

And if you have found yourself in a bumpy patch where nothing seems to be working, step back and ask yourself what *principles* you're striving for here. Are you focusing on the wheels, or are you focusing on the motion and direction of those wheels? Maybe they don't have to be reinvented, but maybe they do need to be smoothed out or altered just a bit. Maybe you need your wheels rotated, or maybe you need an entirely new set.

You will not practice the same way today with your child that you practiced last year, or that you will practice next year. And this is because your child grows, and you grow too. You will change from being 100% involved in the practice to being less involved as your child gains in maturity and skill. This is as it should be!

And because you know your child's full story, you will know how best to adapt for them.

Eat the Fresh Bread

A few years ago, I chose the word WISDOM as my word for the year.
I focused on it that year in the hopes of finding balance, centeredness, mindfulness, and time in my life.

I began taking time out of my day to meditate. I practiced slowing down and thoughtfully considering courses of action before moving on them. I tried self-evaluating and making time for people and relationships, not just goals and personal achievements.

And one magical day, I could tell my practice was actually working. Here's how:

I make homemade bread for my family. It used to be that I would make sure we ate the bread in the order it was baked, so that it was rotated systematically and we weren't left with loaves on the shelf that were super old and dried out. Eat the old loaves first, so nothing went bad or went stale. There was security in knowing that we weren't wasting anything, and that we were eating things in a systematic order.

But, sometimes that meant that even though I'd baked fresh bread and pulled it out of the oven in the afternoon, I'd serve an older, less fresh loaf with dinner.

I was staying organized, thorough, meticulous. Safe.

But here's the thing: I was missing out on fresh bread.

One day I pulled that bread out of the oven and I thought, "This looks delicious and amazing. Why don't I enjoy now, while it's right there in front of me? What harm is there in enjoying this moment?"

And so I did. And it was delicious.

And freeing.

It was a small thing that shifted my paradigm in a big way.

Now when I bake bread, I make sure that my family and I eat at least one of those warm, fresh loaves straight out of the oven, when it's at its best and most delicious. We still get through the other loaves in a systematic way, but we are no longer holding back from enjoying the goodness that is right in front of us.

And I'm taking a lesson from that: go with a little less order, a little more enjoyment, in my life.

Life's short. Eat the fresh bread.

THE PRACTICE: Self-Reflection

1. **Ask yourself the following questions:**
    a. What principles are we seeking in our music study?
    b. Are the ways we are implementing these principles supporting the needs of each individual child in our family?
    c. Is there a way I can change the implementation of these principles to better meet the needs of the individual members of our family?

CONCLUSION: This Will Help You Grow

As you guide your child along their music journey, you're always on the edge of what is mastered and what is a new skill. This is the place of growth: that balance between comfort and discomfort; understanding and questioning; grounding and reaching.

I want, with all the energy of my soul, to reach through these pages and pour in to your heart the feeling that YOU CAN DO THIS. Trust the growth process. If you continue practicing consistency, patience, and just simply showing up and trying, then you and your child will grow in love as you grow in music.

My violin-playing daughter started as a 3-yr-old and we had plenty of tantrums at the beginning of her journey. And I don't mean just from her! It was hard for both of us to get started and to figure out how to work together. But four years later, in a random day of practicing, she paused from her work, turned her bright green eyes up at me and said, "Mom, I love playing the violin."

That did not happen on the first day. And that does not happen every day. But it did happen, and that moment of joy and connection was enough to keep me going one more day after one more day.

Not only has this daughter grown in love of playing the violin, we have, through our hard work together, grown in love for each other.

The magic of the Suzuki method is that it focuses on the growth of the whole child and the development of their heart.

And the secret magic of the Suzuki method is that that growth of the whole person and development of the whole heart that you are seeking for your children *is available to you parents who persevere*. It is not a gift reserved only for your children; it is available for you, waiting to be claimed.

So rise up. Claim it. Be open to the same growth that you are asking of your children. Employ patience, consistency, love, understanding, repetition, and an open heart. Embrace the struggle and its refining powers in to your own life.

EPILOGUE

Parents sometimes jokingly bemoan the fact that children do not arrive on earth with instruction manuals. Wouldn't it just be easier, they ask me, if each child had their own book of instructions, so that the guesswork could be taken out of parenting, and so that we as parents could simply look up the right thing to do at the right time for the right child in the index of some magical book?

I suppose that would be convenient. And I've even longed for it on some of my most challenging days as a parent.

But here's the magic that I want to let you in on: each child *does* in fact come with their own set of instructions. **The guidebook is our children themselves.** The script of their life is being written on their heart word by word, paragraph by paragraph each new day. Each child is the author of their own story, and it unfolds as their life goes along, and as ours goes along with it.

So yes, they do come with their own story and their own instructions, but because the story has just begun, we get to practice patience as we observe the creation of it. Our great challenge comes in sitting in that space of not knowing. Our great privilege is in being witness to its creation.

And that not knowing, that uncertainty, is the beautiful difficulty for us as their parents, their guides. Sometimes we want to make it all better. We want to know the right thing to do at the right time. We want to get through the hard stuff to the good stuff.

But in our desire to mitigate suffering for our children, sometimes we can forget that it's in the experiencing of difficulty that we ourselves have grown, and changed, and become the refined versions of ourselves.

The same is true for our children. The best thing we can do for them is hold their hand and walk by their side during their hard times, their growing times, their joyous times. In short, during the writing of their own story.

So carry on, my fellow parents, and enjoy the privilege it is to watch up close and personally the creation of something so beautiful as your child's life.

This.

This act of trusting, of inhabiting a space of not knowing all the answers but persevering anyway, of giving your all to your relationship with your child even when it feels like it's pulling at your heart, of practicing grace and love while simultaneously extending patience and forbearance.

This.

This will help you grow.

Made in the USA
Middletown, DE
26 April 2022

64755481R00073